A True Love Story Never Ends

Kold Peace

BookLeaf Publishing

India | USA | UK

Presentation by *BookLeaf Publishing*

Web: www.bookleafpub.com

E-mail: info@bookleafpub.com

ISBN: 9789360943455

First edition 2024

This is dedicated to those who have had the experience thus far. You probably think this book is about you… love you! :)

ACKNOWLEDGEMENT

I would like to acknowledge God for making this happen for me. My babies who love me authentically and are what inspire me. To my fam, thank you for the crazy and the love and the unparalleled support.

PREFACE

While on a journey of discovery, writing became the space and time where being true to myself was the easiest. Free from judgments and opinions, I creatively expressed my thoughts and feelings through poetry and journaling. I invite you into my heart and mind, to inspire and motivate others to remain authentically you.

Kold Peace

To be happy in a place that is not welcoming, can be as difficult as running a race and being the only competitor. The incomplete wholeness that remains, the "want to be" that is not the same. So not interested in being a part of that game.

Said & Done

It must have been my co-dependency that lasted for years under the radar.
You being my first had nothing to do with sex, it was more like my first abusive-type ship. First to degrade me, first to hit me, first to embarrass me, and first to brutally injure me. I truly loved and cared for you from the bottom of my heart, only to be your convenience when you were feeling selfish and greedy. Never would I have imagined you thinking that low of me, or the many years of unknown suffering, that you would randomly throw at me. I know I wasn't a winner in your eyes, though you always claim differently. I remained loyal and true to my heart, surely I love you for who you are.

This time moving with caution, but ready to open up. I lost communication and interest in what's required for you. I saw you as my boulder, the thing that stopped me from loving right. One who had me question my heart and if this love thing was going to be alright. The distaste I once felt had been caressed by my genuine care, all while masked by a true love for you.

Intuition

3

Being around you felt so safe, and being with you felt like it was my perfect place. I never understood the hesitation but now I know, this was never meant to be my place, and you never wanted me to know.

Sick and Tired

I want to be sick and tired of not allowing myself to be authentically me, loving and being who I want to be. Sick and tired of not paying attention to the signs, focused on the wrong good times.

Love to Be

5

Only wanting what is meant to be, my happily
ever after until infinity.
Patiently waiting while truly working on me.
Patiently awaiting the authentic and forever true
one for me.
Genuine love orchestrated by destiny, blessed by
the most high.
Always meant to be, spiritually, soul-fulfilling
eternally.

Today

Today I decided to be free.
Today I decided that I wanna have more time for
me.
Today I decided to feel the breeze.
Today I decided to see there is way more beyond
the trees.
Today I decided that I love me much more.
Today I choose me forever and evermore!

The Truth Will Set You Free

Finally getting the chance to see you seemed to
be exciting.
When I saw you, it confirmed that butterflies
were no lie.
I enjoyed the time and the conversations were
great.
Once a hug that could not be touched, now felt
like any other embrace.
With a kiss on the cheek and a soft "thank you",
I finally got the confirmation that we were thru.
Thank you for the closure, it was long overdue.
The lies and deceit are what told me the truth.

True Love

The time alone was just what I needed.
I could not stop smiling when thinking of you.
Believing that you have been chosen to be my
one, I still have doubts that this is happening to
me right now.
Can this be real, or is it just me?
You have been in my face all this time?
Why has it taken so long?
We had to get it right and stop taking control.
Let fate do its thing and leave well enough
alone.
You are mine and I am yours, never to be left
alone again because true love always wins!

Soulful

The soul of my bones shake waiting to have you close to me.
Hugging and kissing all over my insides, teasing me as I cry and moan all over him with you in mind.
She is waiting for you to make it yours, to work on forever and more.
I squeeze tighter and you hold me closer; the deeper you sink in, there is no controlling this ocean.
He smiles while standing up every day, needing to see, kiss, feel, and hug her again somehow, some way.

Cum'n 2 Me

I wanna fuck like a jackrabbit, cumming nonstop.
Don't stop until I pass out, waking back up crying and screaming "Ooooo BABY DON'T STOP!!!"
Keeping me going, sitting pretty, and riding high. Pussy pissing on that D, cumming all up inside!
In need of a remodel, I am sure he can show me right now.
Take your time, and get to know the lay of the land.
Forever being your freaky deaky one, cumming to no end.

Mine's Play'n Trick's On Me

When you touch me, my body gets weak.
When you make love to me, there is no other
love that goes that deep.
Safety and security, you do it without effort.
Hold me in your arms like it is forever!
Mind fucks you so nice, much like dice, I wanna
up my game and mind fuck him twice as nice!

What if...?

What if no one cared, stared into your face as if
you were not there?
What if love was not all it was cracked up to be,
pain and hurt were normal, and the ways things
were meant to be?
What if you were never meant to be "normal",
doing it your way every time, finding
satisfaction in front of jealous eyes?
What if your life was not your own, always
having to be told what you can do and not
having any say about you?
What if life was forever, would you tell him or
her how you felt, or would you brush it off like
it's whatever?
What if I want to sit alone and cry my eyes dry,
to wash away the hate and pain I hold inside?
What if I want to change, leaving behind what
once was, to become and be better than I could
ever imagine?
What if I fall in love with me, and let others do
the same? Learning how great I am and there is
nothing to shame!

Shero (A Mother's Love)

A mother's love is one of a kind.
A mother's love will never leave you behind.
The beauty of this love is like no other.
From one to another, sick and well, for everyone
involved, there is an abundance of loving care.
Motherhood can be hard and at times not selfish.
Motherhood is golden and priceless, sent from
God as a beautiful present.
The strength and energy involved, the care and
concern for many it surrounds.
Like no other superhero I know, for some you
may call her your Shero!

Control is not wanting to let anyone in...

Fear is afraid of which reality?
Fear is what holds you back from being able to move forward with things you can attract.
The fear of the unknown forces the control freak to lose control, stirring up more feelings that make things seem out of control.
Let go of the fear and it will make you see things different, allowing you to see the possibilities that once appeared to be limited.
It is amazing where you could be if you take the blinders off, just for you to see what you should see.
When it comes to health control is good, but not so good when it comes to seeing yourself. When you can't see you because you want to supervise and regulate, who is truly controlling who?

Fuck.Everything.And.Release

15

Just finding the time to free my mind. Tryna find a way to see what needs to be seen, amidst the darkness that tends to creep in. Not sure what is going on, I just wanna continue to win.
Pretty sure I am unsure where I am going, being pulled by my strength to stand tall and continue with all my might. Fear within is what holds us back, knowing it's not right.
Ego holds the brain making you feel like you are going insane. Feelings aren't facts if you just randomly create them, they are mere reactions to things we cannot claim.

The New Knew

I seem to feel you, when no one is there.
You are like my favorite rerun, over and over again.
I think I want you more and more each day.
Thinking of you is my new normal day to day.
Feelings are strong, compassion is stronger.
I know I am yours, no one else matters.
I look forward to getting to know the real you.
This night I pray that all is well with you.
There is a chance that we were meant to be.
Standing in authenticity, I know I love you for me!

I Miss You

I want you, but not ready for you.
I need to feel you, and not sure how to.
You are on my mind, at times, while I try to find
my way.
Times when you are required, but further than a
phone call away.

I'm Ready

Fighting the urge to want you near. Body to body, naked with care. Electric mystical sensations as our souls connect, protected by love and no regrets. Natural fit both inside and out, one so indescribable without a doubt. Picturesque and oh so priceless, love's desire would be so jealous. My love is so limitless, my heart, and my soul I will invest.

Time Has A Wonderful Way of Showing Us What Really Matters

Love is a true testament of the perseverance between two people, and marriage is the solidification of their dedication. Through these years, life experiences and memories finally brought these two together to continue their love story. This story did not start as a once upon-a-time but has a fairytale storyline that is one of a kind.

Those who know them may ask "What took y'all so long?" and others might say "It is about time!" but if you ask them, they will say "It is right on time!". The union seems so perfect, as if it were by design, two souls so parallel it was only a matter of time. As these two prepare to start their journey as one, this day starts the chapter of their together forever after.